PAVING YOUR SUCCESS

A MOTIVATIONAL GUIDE TO SUCCEED

FIROZ TATA

Copyright © Firoz Tata
All Rights Reserved.

ISBN 978-1-64951-491-2

This book has been published with all efforts taken to make the material error-free after the consent of the author. However, the author and the publisher do not assume and hereby disclaim any liability to any party for any loss, damage, or disruption caused by errors or omissions, whether such errors or omissions result from negligence, accident, or any other cause.

While every effort has been made to avoid any mistake or omission, this publication is being sold on the condition and understanding that neither the author nor the publishers or printers would be liable in any manner to any person by reason of any mistake or omission in this publication or for any action taken or omitted to be taken or advice rendered or accepted on the basis of this work. For any defect in printing or binding the publishers will be liable only to replace the defective copy by another copy of this work then available.

Contents

Preface	v
Acknowledgements	vii
1. Sphere Of Happy And Fruitful Life	1
2. Working Towards Self: Motivation For Success	4
3. Setting Up And Accomplishing The Goals	7
4. Recognizing Morals To Achieve The Goals	10
5. Motivation: The Master Of Successful Life	12
6. Managing Stress	14
7. Managing Time	16
8. Maximizing Potential	19
9. Challenging Self Towards Motivation	21
10. Self-limiting Believes To Conquer Hurdles	23
11. Traits Of Human Behaviour To Succeed	25
12. Significant Virtues Towards Success	28
13. Factors Avoiding Success	31
14. Ways To Socialize For Success	33
15. Balancing Personal And Professional Life	35
16. Education And Success	38
17. Developing Inner Self To Face Life Challenges	40
18. Traits Idealizing Successful People	43

Preface

It gives me endless pleasure to bring my writing flair to the frontage by writing this book, 'Paving Your Success'. I am confident that this publication of mine will gratify its purpose and will surely enhance the knowledge to its readers over the habits and techniques to lead happy and successful life.

This book is prepared by keeping in mind the stressful and demanding times we are living in. Stress, demotivation, rejections, failures and over and above expectations have become dominant part of our lives, taking us away from inner peace and happiness. Most of the times people find discouraged, distracted and depressed which stops them to pave their path towards success.

My book is all about 'you' and how you can change your outlook in order to endeavour ahead towards a better and prosperous future. The book will guide its readers step by step the different methods that will help to lead a successful life. After several hours of brainstorming, the chapters are designed in such a way that their reading, understanding and implementations on self will set you towards a newer and brighter direction in life. After all, success is all about having the right shift at the right time.

This book will assist in enhancing and augmenting the knowledge towards self in creating a better and more productive version of you. I have no doubt that this book will be welcomed and appreciated equally by teenagers, ambitious achievers, working class people as well as senior experienced members of the society.

Last but not least, my book aims to inspire the readers to take entire charge of their life in their hands and alter

PREFACE

situations and surroundings accordingly for their advancement. I have tried my level best to use reader-friendly, easy to understand and lucid language throughout the book. Let me assure you that this publication will not only go a very long way in increasing your self-confidence, but will also assist you to discover a beautiful hidden version of you, cultivating a knack to pave the path of long-lasting success.

- The Author

Acknowledgements

From deep down my heart, I would like to express my sincere gratitude to my beloved mother Ms. Heera Tata to once again raise my spirit during the journey of writing this book and providing me with complete isolation while creating it.

I would also love to extend my heartfelt gratitude to Notion Press to provide a beautiful platform of Xpress Publishing, helping me to self-publish this wonderful book on success and motivation for self-improvement and self-enhancement of my readers.

Last but not least, I also want to thank every single individual who says, "You have to buy this book" to their family members, friends and relatives.

- **The Author**

CHAPTER ONE

Sphere of Happy and Fruitful Life

Since childhood we have formed our own definitions of happiness and success. Many of these insights are due to conditioned development, which is a part of our habits due to repetitive inculcation by parents, teachers and society in which we live. Therefore, most of the times none of us can actually ponder about what exactly makes us feel happy and satisfied. This feeling has been left to our sub-conscience and we simply feel the happiness according to the situation we are in.

Several small things in life can give us happiness. For instance, just the thought of doing our favourite morning activity like cycling, walking or running, or even shopping or spending money tends to excite us and makes us feel happy. Various opportunities and positive new notions keep birthing within us to have a similar effect on us. This exciting state makes us imagine things related to these events. For example, the thought of going on a long vacation after receiving an office bonus would not only make us feel excited, but also make us plan and imagine the holidays. In fact, we would feel the bliss and excitement without actually being on the vacation itself. However, when on the actual vacation, gradually the excitement tends to settle down as one begins to feel contented with the environment.

Same is the case with objects. We are quite crazy to purchase the latest products like gadget or even a new car. But once we own that particular stuff, the excitement settles down and the appeal and fondness for the same does not stay the same. However, the cycle of eagerness and excitement begins again when another new product or version is launched in the market.

Let us pause for a second and seriously think about our range of happiness. Is our happiness only dependent on acquiring latest objects? Does it end after our wishes are fulfilled? Is our area of happiness limited to spending good time with family and friends only? We are so involved in this cycle of fulfilling our desires, wishes and hopes that we actually forget to see what real happiness is and how it can be achieved.

The definition of happiness varies from person to person as they have their own individual identities and needs. For some people, achieving a good career path provides happiness and for some it is the completion of goals and objectives. On the other hand, for some, bringing happiness on the face of the poor, needy and deprived people is the real happiness.

However, not all have an easy life. Our income, education, family, friends, health, environment in which we live, society, etc. all determine and affect our happiness. We might not always have the desired income or job needed to fulfil the wishes or may be the career isn't going as smooth as expected. So, how does it affect us? Does it burst our balloons of hopes and excitement or does it renew our hopes, makes us clear about our visions and set ahead for the future with new thrust and motivation? How do we react when things do not turn out as we plan? Most importantly, is our reaction appropriate or do we need to change our approach and perception leading towards happy and successful life?

This book is all about 'you' and how you can change dimensions in order to look ahead for a better and prosperous future. The upcoming chapters are a complete guide to success, setting yourself in a new direction in life. After all, success is all about having the right shift at the right time.

CHAPTER TWO

Working Towards Self: Motivation for Success

In order to be happy and satisfied, one needs to stay focused and motivated. Motivation basically gives us the hope to look ahead and dream better and bigger. It is the force that propels us to go ahead in life. But why do we need to alter? People change for various reasons. Some change because they are tired of their repeated failures. Some change because they do not want to face discomforts and sufferings in lives. For example, poor grades can make a student realize the importance of hard work while studying can motivate us to change. Likewise, debts can make us look for more work or do multiple jobs.

The world is full of negativity and criticism. Irrespective of whatever people say, we need to face this negativity and try to get over it, storming towards our way to success. It is we who has to decide because no one else but only we are in charge of our life, neither others nor the surroundings. Once, we decide that we are in control of our future, we will put our foot down and get over whatever negativity surrounds us.

It is easy for us to remain is the shelter of our comfort zone, but very difficult to step out of it and take a sneak peek into what lies beyond. What exactly prevents you from doing so? Fears? Failure? Shame? or Laziness? The basic thing that we need to improve in ourself is to have a goal and set objectives to accomplish. Once, we know where we are heading towards in life, we will easily maintain our focus, stopping us from being drifted away by anything that obstructs our path towards success.

Next is to set some solid plans that can enable us to strive for our goals. While planning, do not just think within the comfort zone. Step out of the box in order to discover a newer version of you. Identify the problems and boundaries. Use self-discovered techniques to get over them. Make sure that you know what your weaknesses are and strengthen them by controlling the moral standards that you treasure.

Execute your plan and do not worry whether you will succeed or not. Failures should not break you, but rather strengthen you. Constantly devote yourself to transform your plans into reality. If they fail, try to recognise loopholes and use methods which help you overcome them. Every failure teaches us what to avoid and ends in giving a big lesson in life. Learn from these lessons so that you can build and strengthen the newer you.

Try to avoid the birth of negative thoughts. Distant yourself from people who only love to spread pessimism, negativity and discouragement around. Such people hinder the progress and potential, making us go weak and unsuccessful. Trusting on one's own plans and strategies as well as focussing on to change them into reality needs constant hard work, determination and dedication. Regardless of what others say keep working towards your goals and dreams. Such approach will make you jump over the boundaries that block your way towards success.

Last but not least, you need to enjoy life and take things as they come. When you are happy and content, your mind would work faster and triumph will kiss your feet. Thus, chase your visions and take control of your life, setting ahead to enjoy the journey with a newer you.

CHAPTER THREE

Setting up and Accomplishing the Goals

Setting up a goal is a significant part to be successful. It enables to achieve the tasks in an organized fashion and that too within the limited time frame. Hence, it is important that goals are set very carefully. Proper planning is needed for goal setting otherwise one can lose focus and get side tracked. When you set your goals, you do not only feel confident about the work you are doing, but you would also prioritize what needs are to be fulfilled first. This increases motivation and self-esteem leading into positive outlook towards the work.

While setting goals or even planning for them, one has to make sure that goals are reasonable. They should be specific to the point and measurable so that you can judge how much of the goal is accomplished. Goals must be within the limits to achieve. They must be realistic so that they are practically achievable and not vague. Importantly, there should be a time frame in which these goals should be accomplished.

Having a reasonable, wise and smart approach while setting goals would make you identify the flaws and gauge yourself, helping in achieving the goals easily. These goals would help the person to climb the ladder of success in slow but steady way.

When you have a large goal to accomplish, make sure that you divide it into smaller goals making the journey easy while achieving them. For example, if a person has to submit an important report within a deadline, setting smaller goals can help him to achieve larger ones. In this case, steps such as hypothesis, data compiling and result analysis can be the smaller steps which would help to achieve the goal of report submission on time. Deadlines should always be associated with smaller goals so that as you cross them, you are aware of the gradual progress and the work completed.

The major part of goal setting is that it should not be inflexible. Goals should be set such that they are attainable. Flexibility does not mean to be very lenient with the goals, but somewhat, you should bonus up your goal plan as you go along with it. Reinforcing it would make you solve the problems that you face in the implementation of your goal plan. So, time your goals well, perk them up regularly and plan them according to your priorities so that you do not end up losing the set goal.

You can set wide variety of goals in life such as, writing goals, creative goals, professional goals, personal goals, family goals, educational goals, health goals, financial goals, etc. By classifying your lifetime goals, you would be able to make sure that nothing is left behind. Line up your goals so that you know what to prioritize first, when to execute it and when to move to the next goal.

Goal setting not only helps us plan our life, but it also enables us to ensure that we are in a complete control of our life. Therefore, setting smart goals will not only ensure their timely accomplishments but will also make us less apprehensive while achieving them.

CHAPTER FOUR

Recognizing Morals to Achieve the Goals

You might find thought-provoking to know that everyone in this world is managed by morals. Our morals and beliefs are reflected through the decisions we make to lead our lives effectively or ineffectively. We adopt certain morals from our family, school, teachers and sometimes society. At times, some values and morals are already within us, which are seen through our personality traits. Positive values can be adopted at any time in life. A person has to make sure that the value he/she decides to follow has an optimistic, strong and integral effect on life. Since we have to live within a society, it is necessary to adopt such values that meet the demands of society.

Before any other discussion, it is necessary to know the difference between goals and morals. Although morals are not goals, they are interrelated with goals and are highly dependent on them. Goals reflect targets to achieve whereas positive morals and values form that base of a successful life. You need some basis to lead your life. Strong self-belief and actions that drive and support the purpose of our decisions is essential. Effective morals always influence the decisions positively and helps in choosing the right path towards attaining success.

Writing down the morals is a good way to preserve them in life. Thinking for fruitful ways to spend time, writing about right and wrong decisions made in past, considering the aspects of enjoyment and motivation in life or being thoughtful about the actions that may add stability; provides you with an edge to realize what values you possess in life. Moreover, you will be able to differentiate between positive and negative values that influence your life. Writing down the values should be in present tense rather in past tense. For instance, "I am financially stable" than "I will be financially stable". Therefore, all you need is to classify your morals and write them according to your priority. While writing "I am financially stable", one can add other morals like "I clear my bills on time," or "I pay my rent on time".

You can also state your morals in the areas of family, friends, values, community, education, career, health, finances and recreation. Jotting your morals and further classifying them is a time consuming process, but once you are through this, you will surely clear about what your values are and how they influence your actions in life.

Do not hesitate in giving time to identify your morals since they are the foundation on which you set up your goals to accomplish. You become clear about the exact values that influenced your life positively as well as negatively. Sometimes when you are in a state of making a difficult life decision, you certainly need a clear vision of potentials. We already have values instilled within us but writing them down will surely help us to categorize them and set our priorities accordingly.

CHAPTER FIVE

Motivation: The Master of Successful Life

Being successful is very important for everybody. It is the basic need of human beings to gain recognition, dignity, power, position and fame. However, in order to be successful, one needs to be highly disciplined and motivated. Motivation proves to be the inertia and the power to thrive towards success.

- **Following are some of the important reasons that show motivation is needed to succeed:**

(1) Motivation is the fundamental stone towards success: Have you ever been forced to do some work that your heart does not permit? You respond to such work neither passionately nor positively. Now compare such work to some othger work that you like to perform the most. Realize the difference in your attitude when you compare both such tasks. Which one was accomplished quickly with a better outcome? Of course, the task you liked performing the most. This is what motivation is all about. It serves as a start-up so that you can get ahead with the work. The most difficult aspect of any task is to get it started. Once the things get started, there is no turning back. Therefore, motivation is a key factor in making the person get started towards achieving success.

(2) Motivation keeps us going forward: In search of success, a person may not be always rewarded. One has to fall down many times before getting up and moving ahead towards success. Obstacles, after all, are an essential part to make person strong. It makes us worthy of success. So, it is important to be mentally prepared to face the tough work, the challenges and the problems in order to move forward. Keeping yourself motivated all the time in order to keep pushing and going ahead is very important.

(3) Doing little extra: What is it that the successful people do that we do not? People always wondered about this and fails to find the answer. It is what they do extra makes them successful. Even if you have started up, moved on and faced challenges, you still need to push it beyond your normal capacity. Only then one can yield the fruits of sweet success. Doing that extra bit will automatically help the task itself to claim about who has done it.

(4) Life without motivation is dull: Why do we carry books to read or listen to music while going on a long journey? It is to make us feel fresh throughout the journey. Same is in the case with motivation. The road to success is hard, long, laborious, boring and tiresome, but if we have motivation as our companion, then there is no need to worry about anything. Difficult times can be endured by motivation as being motivated ensures that you not only do it the right way, but also enjoy yourself as you keep moving forward. So, always feel motivated, keeping hopes high and looking towards a happier and prosperous future.

CHAPTER SIX

Managing Stress

Stress is the additional tension that a person takes which causes numerous psychological and physiological issues. Thus, it is important to lessen stress as much as possible. Stress management is therefore the relief of stress, essential for everyone to learn. As several factors can cause stress, the elimination of these triggering factors is very important. Stress has a huge impact on the physical health of a person. It can cause hypertension, cardiac problems, common headaches, severe migraine, weight loss or even weight gain. There is no reliable outcome of stress on a person as different people react differently to stress. In some cases, it can even cause fatal cardiac attacks or strokes.

Human beings are creatures of extreme modification. Hence, their reactions to stress management varies to a great extent. Every technique for stress management might not be equally effective for every person. Therefore, one has to discover his/her own personal tool for easing stress.

Primary cause of stress should be assessed before too late. Stress can be related to work or family pressure or any health problem over which one has little or no control. Wrong peers, demanding and inconsiderate life partner, out of control children or excessive work burden can be one of the reasons leading to stress. Work issues such as steep deadlines, annoying boss, gibbering colleagues or a low pay can all enhance stress levels. Thus, one has to discover the factors causing stress so as to be able to control it. It is acceptable that many times, situations are not under control but just knowing what factors causes stress, can make an enormous impact on what method one chooses to alleviate it.

It is said that laughter is the best treatment for any disease. However, one cannot laugh all the time while in stress. Hence, effective methods of stress management should be devised. Some people prefer to have pets like dogs and cats which help them relieve themselves from stress. Some install fish tanks in their home in order to make the environment stress free. Some even use scream therapy, go for jogging, running or cycling, squeeze soft items or take up some hobby so that they can effectively reduce and manage their stress. Energetic physical activities also tend to decrease adrenaline which can reduce stress levels in a person. Adrenaline makes the heart beat faster and increases our energy and ability to move quickly. The last management method to release stress is the use of medications which are prescribed by a specialist doctor. It is recommended that all the stress management techniques should be tried upon before going for medications as these tend to have lots of adverse effects on the body.

To conclude, it is quite important that stress causing factors should be first identified and then lessened through suitable techniques. This would not only help a person to fight against the dangers of stress, but also helps in keeping fit and healthy for a longer period of time.

CHAPTER SEVEN

Managing Time

Having lack of time to do things is the most common complaint that almost everybody has. Initially, time management was considered to be something related for businessmen only. However, nowadays, everybody falls under the sphere of time management. Personal as well as work life can be well organized once a person follows proper time management. However, discipline too is very vital. Efficient time management benefits one's mental and physical health and give them a sense of control and satisfaction. People who are in control of their time actually tend to lead much happy, satisfied and successful lives.

The techniques of time management are not fixed or rigid. Moreover, it is not necessary that all the people get used to all the time management techniques. Therefore, one has to look for the technique that best suits them so that the outcome is maximum. We all tend to practice time management in some way or the other. What needs to be taken care off is how to maximize the effectiveness of our methods.

- **In this chapter we will discuss certain important guidelines for efficient time management:**

(1) Setting up goals and objectives: Whenever you set out to do something, you should be fully aware about the purpose you have to fulfil. This would not only give you a sense of direction, but would also help you to allot specific timings to whatever tasks you have to attain.

(2) Priorities: Set clear priorities in your mind. You should be fully aware of the fact that what is more important to you and what needs to be done immediately. Prioritizing would help you assess your needs and requirements in the long term. The ultimate success of a person depends on how well he/she prioritizes things in life. Short term as well as long term priorities should be made, related to each other. This will eventually help the person to climb the ladder of success. While prioritizing, be stern with those aspects of your time which are not contributing to the long term goals that you have set for yourself. Eliminate those useless areas from your time so that you can fully focus on energizing towards attaining more and more.

(3) Time: While planning your timely needs, make sure to include family and relaxation time in your routine. This will ensure good health and peace of mind. Also, allot sufficient time for meals and exercise to maintain a healthy normal life.

(4) To-do list: Write down your priorities for a particular time period so that you can examine your weaker areas and reinforce the time spent on them. Many people prefer to keep a diary to plan their activities. Several online planners, software, etc. are available so that one can access routine plans from home or from work. However, using the conventional diary is better as it lets you get off the screen for some time and think of your priorities with a peaceful mind. Hence, you can start with baby steps and make a daily to-do list when you start your day. This can slowly enhance the habit of planning everyday routine while you gear up progressively for the full daily time planner mode.

To conclude we can say that time management is surely a more satisfying way to lead successful life. This further helps in controlling what you do to reduce stress while improving health.

CHAPTER EIGHT

Maximizing Potential

We are all talented with a special thing and that is our hidden potential. Some of us realize this potential quite early in life whereas, for some, it takes a lifetime to realize. It is necessary to discover potential on time. People who take time to realize their potential often accept the fact that they have lost their time to bring their real potential to surface. So, it is important to realize the potential within a given time period, else it often gets too late to begin.

One can also realize their hidden flair while discovering their real potential. This is done with growing experience, with the help of family, friends, teachers and even enemies. However, quite unfortunately, people at times, also have a habit to demotivate others to such an extent that their search for the hidden potential is lost in despair.

- **Following are some common strategies that can be adopted to discover and polish our hidden potential:**

(1) Reading: To discover our hidden talent, we can explore through reading things of our interests and stay well-informed of the latest happenings. This will not only keep us updated, but will also make us flourish, especially if we are following a career of our choice.

(2) Finding a good mentor: A successful mentor who understands us would certainly help in discovering our hidden potential. He/she will help us regarding matters such as dealing with family issues, handling peer pressure, business relations and other aspects. A mentor would certainly bring about that hidden talent that yet we ourselves have not realized.

(3) Take challenging work: Taking up different challenges would help in optimizing our potential and find it. Being out of our comfort zone would not only make us realize what we are made up of, but would also surprise us to discover those aspects about personality that are actually unknown to us.

(4) Expand your exposure: Every person needs an exposure to different activities that take place around. In many cases, we realize that our hidden potential lies in the knowledge that we were exposed since childhood. We must travel to places, research various topics of interests and make social contacts with associates that might help in discovering our hidden potential.

(5) Participating in competitions: Participating in various competitions helps to plunge into our own pool of talent and invent the things that are yet not invented. However, this would consume much time and energy, but will enhance our skills.

(6) Attempt new things: Treat every day as a new day and a new beginning. Look ahead at new avenues and do not hesitate to try new things or take risks.

To conclude, every one of us has unique potentials hidden within. All we need to do is to wake up and start discovering them.

CHAPTER NINE

Challenging Self Towards Motivation

The initiative of having a goal oriented behaviour is the result of motivation. The actual purpose of motivation is to decrease the mental or physical stress and increase the reasons of happiness in a person. Intrinsic and extrinsic are the two types of motivation. The intrinsic motivation is that which is displayed through delight in a given situation. Such motivation is within the individual itself. On the other hand, extrinsic motivation is that which is exhibited or enhanced by external factors such as money, reinforcements, gifts or pressure.

If a person is strongly motivated to achieve or gain something huge in life, then that person involves in aiming high for the future. This is the reason why motivation is intertwined with challenges. Moreover, we are physically and mentally designed in such a way that we are always ready to accept and face different challenges.

Motivation can be explained further by one of the following circumstance. If, for instance, one comes to know that he/she is in danger, then the immediate response would be to take all the necessary precautionary measures in order to prevent themselves from the danger to ensure safety. As such situation challenges one's security and life, it manages to increase one's motivation towards the act of protecting themselves. In this manner, we need to engage ourselves in various challenges so that our confidence and impetus remain boosted. Facing and overcoming the challenges tends to impart a positive feeling that increases one's motivation. It also makes us test our patience and to what extent we can stretch ourselves.

The best way to deal and involve in challenges in our lifestyle and daily routine is by setting goals and trying to accomplish them successfully. A person's general character and personality are formed through learning and practicing the standards and ethics of the social culture. However, as all the values do not have a positive influence on us, one must have a correct frame of mind full of motivation so that it becomes easy to create our own values and live accordingly. Constant reconditioning of inner self would let person see everything as a challenge and undergo the change of values that are needed. Too much relaxing of the brain would make a person feel like a lazy idler. Thus, it is healthier to keep the brain busy and in action.

It might be tiring to keep yourself up to the challenges that life throws all the time but when we become use to it, we can master the skills of being motivated and successful.

CHAPTER TEN

Self-limiting Believes to Conquer Hurdles

In the words of Michael Jordan, *"Obstacles don't have to stop you. If you run into a wall, don't turn around and give up. Figure out how to climb it, go through it, or work around it."*

Life is definitely difficult than it seems to be. Although we tend to face problems and hurdles at every phase of life, we know that we have to look ahead and keep moving. The hurdles can be in the form of family conflicts, financial problems, health related issues or problems connected to adjustment in social life. All of these are actually related to the self-limiting beliefs that stop us from moving ahead.

The smallest awareness can create a belief which gradually grows bigger. Many times we tend to become unconscious and direct all the actions in accord with these self-formed beliefs. These unintentional acts tend to slowly become a part of our character and habit, resulting in a huge impact on our personality. When we talk about such beliefs, they can be of various types. There are many beliefs which have a tendency to create a positive impact on our personality and lifestyle. However, in some cases, these beliefs can be negative and tend to create a huge impact on our personality, making us feeble.

When facing such obstacles, one has to deal with perseverance and courage. The stronger we remain, lesser they will appear big; helping us to conquer them.

- **Following are the ways to deal with such obstacles:**

(1) Optimistic thinking: Optimistic approach and thinking is the first step towards hurdling your obstacles. The thought of quitting a task would never let a person succeed. Thus, a positive mindframe is necessary at all the times in order to find solutions to problems and obstacles you face. Optimistic attitude not only lets you have a clear thinking mind, but also helps in what you want to achieve.

(2) Relax your mind: Tension and stress never lets a person succeed in life. Being tension free would make you focus more so that maximum obstacles are eliminated.

(3) Determination: The problem will be never solved on its own without you being focused and determined to solve it. You need to wait for the outcome of results and for that patience and endurance is an experience in itself, which passes through the test of time. This will make you have a whole new vision about the concept of the problem.

(4) Find new opportunities: Vitality is the key to success. So do not wait for opportunities to show up. Rather, take charge, find new challenges and create your own window of opportunities in life. It will not only make you creative, but will also make you determined and strong.

(5) Inspiration: The aspect of inspiration is the wish or dream that makes you work harder and overcome obstacles. Inspiration gives the spark that one need to propel ahead towards a higher future.

CHAPTER ELEVEN

Traits of Human Behaviour to Succeed

Motivation is the reason which instils people to embark upon certain behaviour that is influential in nature. This convincing nature tends to motivate people towards that particular task, goal or objective. Therefore, motivation is the force that drives an individual and propels them towards their objectives and success.

In order to be motivated, one has to adapt a certain behavioural patterns that actually trains the mind to work energetically. Thus, it is a state of mind which is not related to one's personality but is rather adopted by a person, who is essentially motivated.

- **Following are certain aspects of behaviours that tend to drive a person towards being motivated:**

(1) Stimulation of behaviour: This is the triggering factor that brings a change of mind. A motivated person tends to start thinking about the actions related to what motivated them. These actions arouse one's behaviour in which certain action plans are created in the mind of the person who is motivated.

(2) Direction of behaviour: Direction of behaviour is the position of one's thoughts and actions so that a sense of direction is formed. When a person's behaviour is directed, he/she tends to maintain focus towards targeted objective. Moreover, direction also maintains one's thoughts towards that particular plan of action.

(3) Determination of behaviour: Determination is an important element in motivation. It ensures continuity and concreteness pertaining to the action plans. It maintains the levels of one's motivation and also continues the goal achievement of the person.

Other than these behavioural aspects, motivation is also catered by some motives that are important. These motives can be psychological or physiological in nature. These motives fall under the category of homeostatic motives, non-homeostatic motives and social motives also called learned motives. Homeostatic motives include air, thirst, hunger, etc. These motives are essential for one's existence. Non-homeostatic motives include shelter seeking habits, curiosity to know, etc. Social motives include approval, appreciation, etc.

Homeostatic elements are innate and do not need nurturing. They are present as an inherent part of human nature. Non-homeostatic elements tend to be affected by the surroundings and can arise due to general observation. However, social or learned motives are different in every individual as people tend to behave differently, face variety of challenges and are moulded continuously by the people and the situation around them.

Individual's response to these motives varies from person to person. Responses depend on the upbringing, experience and learning pattern of a person. Therefore, every individual responds differently when feels motivated.

However, responses are displayed through the behavioural traits and the motives followed.

The key point to remember is, no matter how a person is habituated, he/she must always respond positively to maximize the potential and develop motivation. Once we learn how to control these behavioural aspects, we can take charge of ourselves and alter sails according to the direction life drives us in. This will help to move easily in to the lands of opportunities and success.

CHAPTER TWELVE

Significant Virtues Towards Success

We often wonder how a person can be so successful in life. Is it because he inherits success or is it because he possesses a unique character? The answer to such questions are, the existence of certain important personality virtues that we can adopt in order to be successful in life.

- **These virtues are as follows:**

(1) **Genuineness:** Being sincere and following values and beliefs with complete discipline, dedication and devotion would guarantee success. Thus, do not try to be something that you aren't. Just be your original self and impress others through good deeds.

(2) **Being passionate:** One should be passionate and enthusiastic regarding things they do. A person should enthusiastically apply self to do good to others and community.

(3) **Sympathy:** Always be kind and sympathetic to people under emotional stress and discomfort. Try to understand things from their perspective.

(4) Earnest: Be honest and appreciate others. Thank people who do good to you. Reach out to those in distress.

(5) Cheerful: Be warm, welcoming and sincere with people you meet. This would further emit your charm and affection towards them.

(6) Humbleness: No matter how rich or successful a person is, always be humble with others. This would have a long lasting impression and impact on others. Such individual gains more and more love, respect, approval and appreciation.

(7) Principled: Share your skills, insight, time and knowledge to those in need. This will help them to grow in life and learn from your experience. Avoid low and short thinking that they will get ahead of you in life. However, for this it takes a high mentality and a generous heart.

(8) Wisdom: Wisdom multiplies with experience. Be in constant touch with your inner self in order to gain higher understanding and wisdom.

(9) Incorruptibility: Be assenting and hold your opinions and stick to your firm beliefs. Do not let others corrupt your values and change your mind.

(10) Good decision: Treating everybody with equality and admiration is very essential. Showing good and fair judgment through various decisions in life is a sign of a good person.

(11) Charity: Be generous and charitable to others. Extend your helping hand even to those who have not helped you in life.

(12) Focused: Maintain full focus and give your total attention on the work you do and the people you interact.

(13) Courteousness: Being nice and decent to others and showing courtesy even to strangers who have never done any good to you is a fine virtue that a person can have.

(14) Be upfront: Always remember, actions speak louder than words. Exaggerating or deceiving people, blocks the long-term path towards success. Just be upfront about what you exactly feel in a particular given situation.

(15) Authentic: Being authentic is quite difficult and challenging, but when you let honesty show you the way, you will achieve greater success in life. Deceiving is not the way to get ahead in life.

(16) Empathy: Know that everybody is different and has different desires and needs. Comprehend with the feelings and thoughts of others.

(17) Integrity: It is important that no matter how rich and successful you become, you should always keep those believes, morals and values intact. Never trade your morals for material gains.

(18) Compassionate: Reach out and help those who are in anguish. You wouldn't believe the invisible blessings and good wishes their hearts will shower out to you.

(19) Selflessness: Think for others and their needs without being selfish. Do good and don't expect things in return. Moreover, never express to others the favours you do to them.

The traits mentioned above are some of the assets that a successful person always possess. Try to adopt and make them a part of your life and nature, helping you to climb the ladder of success in life.

CHAPTER THIRTEEN

Factors Avoiding Success

In order to be successful, following are certain factors that a person must definitely avoid, only then it can ensure success.

(1) False beliefs: Any wrong or inaccurate idea that one possesses about something is regarded as a false belief. The best step towards success is to let go false beliefs by getting over them and moving ahead. A small false belief such as being unlucky or not able to find a job should not stop you from looking for a job. To get over false beliefs, one needs to step out of their comfort zone and accept challenges so that they can overcome their false beliefs and move on towards newer horizons.

(2) External control: A specific way of thinking which is strongly associated with being unsuccessful is blaming everything to external factors. For example, when one does not perform well in an exam, he blames his teacher or the surroundings around him. On the other hand, a successful person reverts to self to control and believes that he is responsible for failure. Such person strengthens himself internally so that he can face all the challenges that life throws.

(3) Inflexibility: Unsuccessful people are quite inflexible. They tend to stick to their outdated ways and do not like adapting themselves to the changes. However, in modern times, one needs to be highly flexible in order to be successful. A person needs to adapt to situations accordingly and try different methods if he/she fails.

(4) Improper planning: Being planned for future would guarantee success. If we have our plans, we will maintain our focus in the correct direction. Those who are unsuccessful do not plan or even if they do, their plans have loopholes and remain incomplete. Thus, appropriate planning is very essential or else one can be easily swept away by those around.

(5) Lack of self-confidence: Think why unsuccessful people are always left behind? It is all because of the lack of self-confidence in presenting their ideas. It is always good to speak up, be creative and give ideas so that people around realize that you are a confident person.

(6) Keep pondering about lack of means: A lot of unsuccessful people stay behind just because they think that they do not possess enough money or the resources to do things. If an affirmative and determined approach towards success is adopted, a person will have to find his way out without resources.

(7) Fears: These are the fears which obstruct our ability to dive ahead towards success. However, the fear of success or failure can both hinder the way towards being successful. Thus, overcoming fears and starting to move ahead is the best possible thing a person can do.

CHAPTER FOURTEEN

Ways to Socialize for Success

Having a quality friend circle and socializing is a great way to drive your life ahead. It is not always that we come across people whom we get on well with. However, having an active social life is a great way to keep ourselves encouraged. Spending quality time with certain people not only makes our mood elevated, but it also enhances our emotional wellbeing and overall personality. It is important to understand that one should not only make a lot of friends, but rather, be friends with those who are unbiased, progressive and ambitious. Positive people tend to have a lot of positive influence on our life.

However, while making social links, it is important that we realize some social habits that would be harmful for our social relations. Such habits should be completely avoided.

- **Following things should be implemented while socializing with progressive social circle:**

(1) Talking about motivation and passion of others: A good social asset for all times is to talk about the social possessions of others as much as possible. This would make you find out what inspires them the most and how they tend to be so naturally motivated. You can discuss their passions and ask them why they are so fascinated towards them. As the person gets better in this skill, he will realize that at times, he can even discover somebody's hidden potentials that even they are unaware off.

(2) Complaint and whining: Whining is a major no. It is highly negative and a red flag for those with whom you socialize. It makes social circle dislike you. Even though you might think that you do not really complain, people around you might be more sensitive about this issue. Realize the fact that how much people around you suffer from your grumbling habit and how often you do it.

(3) Blowing one's own trumpets: Boasting and blowing one's own trumpets might be very satisfying and happy experience. It boosts our ego for a while, but actually tends to be quite damaging for our social circle. However, nobody prefers to be in the company of a boaster and it often leaves a bad impression on people you socialize with. Only if you are a comedian and are boasting for fun, then it is surely to be taken in a cheerful manner.

However, a person needs to learn the difference between honesty and boasting. If you are honestly telling others about your achievements, then there is no need to hide them. Rather, if you actually feel like telling others about something, then that is supposed to be boasting. So assess yourself on these parameters and try to judge about where you go wrong while socializing with people. Correct yourself and use these knowledgeable guidelines so as to appropriately interact with people and move towards a positive personal change.

CHAPTER FIFTEEN

Balancing Personal and Professional Life

The world is changing rapidly and one has to work in order to live a better life. In this race of survival, one often mixes up their personal and professional life. This results in a topsy-turvy life, messed up priorities, lack of time management, increase in stress and overall dissatisfaction. This also gives a feeling to the person that despite all the hard work, one still has something missing in life. This missing element is the mental harmony that one needs to focus in life.

It is therefore advisable that a person must follow certain rules in order to keep his/her life simple, uncomplicated and healthier with a balance between the personal and professional life. However, some of these factors are in our control where as some may be out of the spheres of our control.

(1) Work balance:

(a) Taking short breaks during the day is always preferable. Break taken every couple of hours increases the effectiveness and work productivity can be enhanced.

(b) Prioritizing the day and dividing the time sincerely is must.

(c) Pending work of office should not be carried home.

(d) Difference between personal and professional life should be learnt. Working or thinking about work 24/7 badly disturbs health and personal life.

(e) Deal appropriately with unrealistic deadlines before it is too late. Communicating problems with boss avoids stressful issues at later stages.

(f) Use your much deserved leaves and vacations so that you can return fresh at work again.

(2) House balance:

(a) Relaxing and spending good time with family after returning from work is always cherished by all.

(b) Equally distributing domestic tasks amongst family members helps the family to sit together and share some quality memorable time.

(c) Exercising for at least twenty minutes a day creates wonders on mind and body. Moreover, it energizes and refreshes the person.

(d) Eating healthy diet on correct time helps increasing productivity of a person in general.

(e) Adopting a hobby that can be pursued with family or friends is wonderful. This would keep our mind off work and also makes us much more motivated. Hobbies are effective in alleviating stress.

(3) Community balance:

(a) Spending some quality community time feels great. Devote yourself in community works by offering money, knowledge and your time for social causes. This would enhance your satisfaction level and creates a sense of social responsibility. You can also generate funds and help in organizing charitable social events. In this way one can use their maximum capacity to give back to community.

(b) One can also participate in children's school events and parental groups in order to know what your child is learning at school. Parental groups are also involved in organizing functions and social events for the school kids. This would not only help in managing your time, but will also impart such delightful social habits in your children.

CHAPTER SIXTEEN

Education and Success

Education is regarded as one of the fundamental values on which one's success highly depends. To understand the role of education in attaining success, one has to first understand how it influences a successful life. A successful life can be claimed by person's wealth, fame, career, assets and most of all, personality. According to many, one needs to have luck for success. Those who are born with wealth are already successful. However, the truth is that being born with assets will not make us a successful person until we prove ourselves to be worthy of it.

So irrespective of the fact whether a person is born rich or poor, he needs to focus on how he can be successful and how he can maintain the position. Now comes the question, why do people lay more emphasis on being educated in order to be successful? Well, it is quite simple. Education gives you the sense of direction, the knowledge, the skills and the focus which is needed in order to be successful. Moreover, good foundation is also important as many who have succeeded in their career paths have done so because they took correct decisions at correct time. Our decisions heavily depend on our education and level of experience.

Highly educated entrepreneur and an average uneducated businessman have different methods, strategies, viewpoints and planning tendencies towards business. Moreover, education makes us stand out amongst the others, gives an edge, self-respect and elegance. The chances of having a better paid job and even a better career heavily depend on our level of education.

College dropouts such as Bill Gates of Microsoft, Michael Cell of Dell Computers and Steve Jobs of Apple are some of the exceptional examples who were so intelligent and hardworking that lack of education did not stop them to be successful. But following their path is not everybody's cup of coffee as we have to face the reality rather than dreams. Despite not having a college degree, these great men were so brainy, that they become billionaires. However, not everybody can follow the footsteps of these exceptional men as all do not have the required intelligence or luck in order to make it as big as them.

We cannot just sit down and keep dreaming. The best thing to do is take charge of self and perceive education. A Masters or any professional degree is great. These degrees would not only land us in better paying jobs, but also make us worthy of it. Our personality and values are moulded by the education we get. Education helps us to deal with occupational and business situations and decisions that otherwise leave us disorganized and disordered. Moreover, our innersoul would also be fortified through education. The values that education give us, would also help us to portray our self in a much better way in society.

Therefore, good education is the key to success as it transforms our knowledge, values and our outlook towards the path to success.

CHAPTER SEVENTEEN

Developing Inner self to Face Life Challenges

Everything begins from our mind. The smallest thought generated in mind changes into an idea, which takes the shape of an action in order to be applied. This whole process is functioned within one's mind to plan ahead. Therefore, positivity is an important thinking approach that all successful people have. We have all been kindly granted with positivity inside us. It is a matter of choice for those who want to use it or not. People who are positive in their approaches attract us more than those who are negative and always blames others or their environment for the failures.

Our thought processes are controlled by our mind. These processes are reflected and exhibited by our behaviour, attitude and insight. It also shows the type of lifestyle we would prefer. Those who are happy tend to have positive thinking which emits around them. However, those who are gloomy have negative aura that emits around them. Hence, it is up to us as to what type of lifestyle we prefer, positive or negative.

Happiness and misery, both are important elements of life. No matter how wealthy one is, one can certainly never avoid neither happiness nor misery. These problems which encircle us tend to make us stronger internally as they teach us about life, about values and how to face different challenges that we come across in our daily routine. It is generally seen that those who face their life challenges positively have positive outcomes where as those who face challenges with a negative attitude, usually end up with negative results.

- **Following are some of the important guidelines which will help you to improve your day-to-day routine and develop inner self:**

(a) When facing negative thoughts, try to change them into positive ones. Always remember that you can control your thoughts, your thoughts should not be controlling the way you live.

(b) Instead of complaining and accusing others, assess your options. Think of the best possible solution under the given circumstances and act accordingly upon them.

(c) Do not hang out with negative people. Stay in the company of those who think positively. Talk or get counselling with people who tend to think positively and are a source of inspiration for you.

(d) Find happiness in simple things in life. Remember to look upon the less fortunate and deprived people. Be grateful for what you have.

(e) Love yourself instead of blaming. Be kind and respect others. Do small gestures of kindness such as a simple smile and hello to people around. The positive signals you send out are met with positivity in response which increases your satisfaction level.

(f) Help the unfortunate ones. Give some voluntary service to those in need. Spend time with the people living in misery and release your positivity onto them.

To conclude we can say, we get what we give. So send indications of positivity and give hopes to others. Do remember that when you give others a reason to smile for and hopes to cherish, you will get the same in return.

CHAPTER EIGHTEEN

Traits Idealizing Successful People

We have many aspirations and dreams. Throughout the various stage of growing up, we tend to idealize important people in our life. They can be our favourite sportsmen, movie stars, teachers or family members. This gradual idealism leaves an impact on us. Gradually, our personality reflects certain traits of our ideals which we have absorbed from them in the due course of time.

Not all individuals are worthy of idealism. It also depends upon how we see ourselves. A thief would always idealize his gang leader, not the local priest. Hence, if we aspire to be worthy and successful individual in life, then we need to idealize certain people who have the following important traits.

(1) Values time: Successful people value their time. They are well prioritized and planned. They also value the time of others and fulfil their deadlines effectively.

(2) Positive attitude: A positive attitude not only makes us successful, but it also makes us open to all the opportunities that come our way. Successful people have positive vibrations and they never let go of any opportunity. Grabbing minute opportunities with both hands helps them to climb their success ladder.

(3) Creative: Creativity is yet another key to success. Creativity helps in opening new windows of opportunities. All the leaders and successful people are supposed to be creative. Their creativity makes them implement certain changes that are required for a turnover of the organization.

(4) Resilience: Success do not come without failures. Being successful is not a piece of cake. It takes a lot of dedication, constant hard work, determination and resilience. The strength needed to stand up after failing is the real test that successful people go through. This means that resilience, as a trait, should never be overlooked while selecting successful ideals. A person cannot be successful if he/she has not undergone any setbacks.

(5) Practical: Being well planned is the key trait of successful people. They are practical in their actions and their positive attitude supports their practical measures.

(6) Well communicated: In modern times, good and fluent communication skills is an important asset of successful individuals. Being well versed in the verbal and non-verbal communication skills reflects hugely upon the personality of a successful individual. Reaching out to others through good interaction can attract a lot of people who may also bring newer opportunities.

(7) Answerability: Despite being high risk takers, successful people tend to be answerable for their actions, shortcomings and even failures. If by chance they fail, they do not blame their environment or other people.

Above mentioned traits are just a few traits that successful people possess. These traits are quite worthy and one can look for them while selecting their ideals.

www.ingramcontent.com/pod-product-compliance
Lightning Source LLC
LaVergne TN
LVHW021739060526
838200LV00052B/3366